W9-DFW-834

THE FIVE HUNDRED BEST ENGLISH LETTERS

THE FIVE HUNDRED BEST ENGLISH LETTERS

Selected and Edited,
with an Introduction,
by

THE FIRST EARL OF BIRKENHEAD

CASSELL AND COMPANY LIMITED
LONDON, TORONTO, MELBOURNE
AND SYDNEY

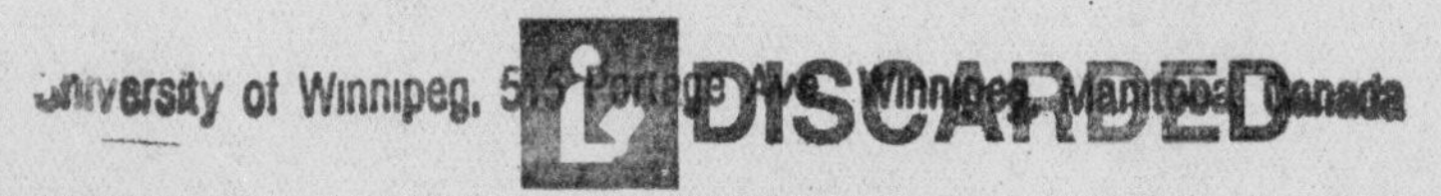

First published, 1931

PRINTED IN GREAT BRITAIN

DEDICATED TO

OLIVER LOCKER-LAMPSON

It was my Husband's wish that this book
should be dedicated to his great friend

Margaret Birkenhead

INTRODUCTION

I ENDEAVOURED in a previous volume ("Law, Life and Letters") to appraise in some measure the claims of various literary letter-writers. The material before me then was the work of professionals. It consisted of compositions, casual and perhaps unpremeditated, but still coming from pens accustomed to perform for the public. Actors, even when off the stage, still preserve some of the arts with which they beguile their audiences during their performance; accustomed, if I may use their highly expressive jargon, to get it across the footlights, they put into action some of the same, or analogous devices when exerting themselves to get it across the dinner-table. The mask and buskin are never completely discarded. So it is with writers. Pen in hand, they are accustomed to address a contemporary public, whose exact degree of attention they can undoubtedly measure, and a future posterity, concerning whose attitude to themselves they are as uncertain as they are hopeful. This habit is strong, and rules them even when they use the post for purposes purely domestic or personal. They cannot, without doing some violence to their acquired characters, be unbuttoned, at their ease, and their own familiar selves. Their letters, even when they do not smell of the lamp, have a slightly artificial perfume. They are rarely "native wood-notes wild."

The letters collected in this volume must not be judged as a collection of the rarest flowers. I have not here chosen among only the most ambitious or consummate examples of the epistolary art. The principle of selection adopted by me has a different range. There will indeed be found in this collection masterly pages, or pages by the hands of masters. But their presence is fortuitous. My aim has been rather biographical and historical. I have selected from each century representative letters written by representative men and women, thus endeavouring to hold up a mirror to the past. I have tried to make each century speak in the shape of its representative men, and each representative man or woman speak in his or her most authentic voice. If literary men, professionals of the pen, have insinuated themselves into this company, I have only admitted them when they were off their guard, and had, momentarily at least, forgotten their literary stilts.

It is a common observation, patent to even incult and untrained minds, that each period of history has an unmistakable character of its own. It is rather profounder and subtler to observe that similar characteristics run through the products of each. The same general remarks and descriptive epithets applicable to the cathedrals of each period are applicable to its clothes. Letters form no exception to this rule. Beginning as this selection does (except for the first letter) about the time that English began to be used in England, almost every letter could at once be placed in the century to which it belongs as surely as a manor-house or bygone fashion in dress, even if it were unsigned and undated. There can be no doubt to what time such writing as this took place. To take two examples:

"Like as the riche man that dayly gathereth riches to riches, and to one bag of money layeth a greate sort til it come to infinit, so me thinks, your Majestie not beinge suffised with many benefits and gentilnes shewed to me afore this time, dothe now increase them in askinge and desiring wher you may bid and commaunde, requiring a thinge not worthy the desiringe for it selfe, but made worthy for your highness request.'

Again:

"To reckon up all parts of knowledge, and to show the way to attain to every part, is a work too great for me at any time, and too long to discourse at this; therefore I will only speak of such knowledge as your lordship should have desire to seek and shall have means to compass."

Intentional parody could not be more characteristic of the times. Such a passage might almost be found in *Love's Labour's Lost*, and might well have flowed from the pen of Holophernes. There is no mistaking the gorgeous magnificence, the lavish elaboration, the moral sententiousness; equally discernible in a Holbein portrait or in the stone-work of Inigo Jones. We are without doubt in the ampler times of Great Elizabeth.

Nor is error possible in dating the following:

"The Count Dampier had some twelve days since taken from the Hungarians, by surprise in the field, thirteen cornets of horse, and one ensign of foot, which here with much ostentation were carried up and down, and laid on Sunday was seven night under the Emperor's feet, as he came from Chapel. Some note that the vanity of this triumph was greater than the merit: for the Hungarians, by their ordinary discipline, abound in cornets, bearing one almost for twenty horse, so as flags are good cheap amongst them, and but slightly guarded."

Or this direction, as to the manner in which children should be brought up.

"Breed them up in a love one of another. Tell them it is the charge I left behind me. Tell them it was my counsel, they should be tender and affectionate one to another. For their learning be liberal, spare no cost. Rather keep an ingenuous person in the house to teach them than send them to schools, too many evil impressions being commonly received there."

The first was written by Wotton, the second by William Penn; two distinguished men, but not in the first rank of authors. They are stamped with the marks of a later and more classic age; they are marked by a lucid simplicity, a dignity without artifice, and an austere moral elevation that belongs only to the age of Wren and Milton; the florid exuberance of the past has been pruned, the pedestrian dryness of the next age has not yet come. And it is only in that next age, in the Eighteenth Century, that we could expect to read in a letter phrases such as these:

"They write, that you are not only *decrotté*, but tolerably well-bred;

and that the English crust of awkward bashfulness, shyness, and roughness (of which, by the bye, you had your share) is pretty well rubbed off. I am most heartily glad of it; for as I have often told you, these lesser talents of an engaging, insinuating manner, a genteel behaviour and address, are of infinitely more advantage than they are generally thought to be, especially here in England."

Compare the following passage, also dealing with the education of children, with the one already quoted and written a hundred years later. How much the habits of the mind have changed in a period of time relatively short!

"Perhaps you may have more success in the instructing your daughter; she has so much company at home, she will not need seeking it abroad and will more readily take what you think fit to give her. As you were alone in my family, it would have been thought great cruelty to suffer you no companions of your own age, especially having so many near relations, and I do not wonder their opinions influenced yours. I was not sorry to see you not determined on a single life, knowing it was not your father's intention."

We have been transported into the age of social politeness and reasonable common sense.

The letters of the Nineteenth Century are equally characteristic; but we are too close to discern its features as unmistakably. It is easier to parody others than ourselves.

Each age has its characteristic form of art. Material conditions dictate the form, and one is really not better than the other. Great urban crowds with high wages, mechanical invention and a mass production of popular entertainment have produced the Films. Unfortunately we are reluctant to admit new forms of art, and a new form when popular is suspected of vulgarity, and even of demoralizing the public. This is one example of the pedantry that blights art; it is forgotten that the theatre, long ago admitted into respectability and academic honour, once lay under the same suspicion. Now letter-writing as an art is fading out, just as the theatre is declining. Conditions are against it. Urban life (and characteristic modern life is urban), offers too many distracting alternatives of action and amusement to everybody. There are, again, too many ways of communicating rapidly with each other; this is another result of the mechanical inventions that have created urban life. But life in Europe used to be a country life. We read about towns in the past, and see them marked on maps, but they only dotted the vast surface of tillage, pasturage, and wood; the capitals themselves contained residences of the wealthy, ascending by degrees of splendour to the glories of a kingly court, in which life still resembled what we call a country life. We have parks because English Kings could not be without their hunting. Our ancestors had a standard of culture, higher in many respects than ours. In theory our vanity prevents us from recognizing it; but in practice every one who can afford to live in a house or sit on a chair, made by them, is obliged to do so. Our ancestors were, however, separated from each other by distances not to be measured by miles. They could not often meet; they had time on their hands. The building of roads brought the post into existence, and the post a new form of communicative art; just as the use of selenium has brought the Talkie to birth. The post gave cultured, separated, leisured people a fresh impulse towards self-expression, and stimulus towards friendship. They took as much interest in their letters as we do in cars.

I doubt if history, as written and talked, always gives us the true impression of past life. It is often too abstract. We may know the map of Spain in all its details. A few hours spent in a Spanish town or with a Spanish novel may give us fresher and more faithful facts.

I venture to think a batch of letters from any century reveals what life was, more vividly than the laborious compilations of the erudite. Sometimes they bring the flame of genius to bear on it; though that flame often discolours the past with its own passions, political, social or religious. It is the historian who talks to us out of the history book, not the post. Letters leave an impression that is not abstract, and therefore never dull; not second-hand, and therefore not misleading. In their letters the men of the past are still speaking to us as they spoke to each other; and when we read an old letter from one of them we undergo much the same impression as the correspondent did at the time; if we have a little knowledge of the circumstances in which it was written, we may even share the response of the recipient.

In this selection the reader moves from century to century. I hope he will find every item entertaining in itself. In any case he can be sure that broken and intermittent as may be the lights which these letters throw upon the "dark, infinite, backward abyss of time," they reveal yesterday in its truth.

ACKNOWLEDGMENTS

THE Editor and Publishers desire to make acknowledgment to the following publishers and owners of copyrights for their kind consent to the inclusion of the respective items in this book:

George Allen & Unwin, Ltd., Lord Acton, from *Letters of Lord Acton to Mary Gladstone*; Elizabeth Fry, from *The Gurneys of Earlham.*

Edward Arnold & Co., Lady Mary Sibylla Holland, from *Letters of Lady Mary Sibylla Holland*; Lord Lyons and Sir Edward Malet, from *Life of Lord Lyons*, by Lord Newton.

George Bell & Sons, Ltd., Lady North, from *Lives of the Norths*; Coventry Patmore, from *Memoirs and Correspondence of Coventry Patmore.*

Ernest Benn, Ltd., Gertrude Bell, from *The Letters of Gertrude Bell*; Lewis Carroll, from *The Life and Letters of Lewis Carroll*; Edward Lear, from *The Letters of Edward Lear to Lord Carlingford* and *Later Letters of Edward Lear*; T. Sydenham, from *The Life of Thomas Sydenham.*

A. & C. Black, Ltd., John Ruskin, from *Letters of Dr. John Brown.*

Basil Blackwell, Lieut. Heath, from *Letters of Arthur Heath.*

Thornton Butterworth, Ltd., Winston Churchill, from *My Early Life*, by the Rt. Hon. Winston S. Churchill.

Cambridge University Press, E. V. Lucas, from *Cambridge and Charles Lamb.*

Chapman and Hall, Ltd., John Constable, from *The Letters of John Constable.*

Chatto and Windus, Alfred and Henry VIII, from *Kings' Letters* in the "Kings Classics" Series.

Constable & Co., T. E. Brown, from *The Letters of Thomas Edward Brown.*

Gerald Duckworth & Co., Ltd., W. S. Landor, from *Letters of Walter Savage Landor, Private and Public.*

Victor Gollancz, Ltd., Lieuts. Eversden and Donaldson, Capt. Sir Edward Hulse, from *War Letters of Fallen Englishmen.*

W. Heffer & Sons, Ltd., Gawdy letters and F. Willis, from *Early Collegiate Life*, edited by Dr. J. Venn.

John Hogg, for permission to use the letters of Thomas De Quincey.

John Lane the Bodley Head, Ltd., T. L. Beddoes, from *The Letters of Thomas Lovell Beddoes*; Mrs. Vesey, from *Bluestocking Letters.*

Longmans Green & Co., Ltd., the Carlyles, from *Carlyle's Early Life* and *Carlyle's Life in London*; Lord Macaulay, from *Life and Letters of Lord Macaulay*; Mandell Creighton, from *Life and Letters of Mandell Creighton*; Nanny Fox, from *Irish Memories*, by E. Œ. Somerville and Martin Ross; Sir George Cornewall Lewis, from *Letters of Sir George Cornewall Lewis*; M. Rodes and John Tomkins, from *Letters from a Quaker Post-bag.*

Macmillan & Co., Ltd., Edward Fitzgerald, from *Letters of Edward Fitzgerald*; Matthew Arnold, from *Letters of Matthew Arnold*; Florence Nightingale, from *Life of Florence Nightingale*; Thomas Hardy, from *The Later Years of Thomas Hardy*; Lord Randolph Churchill, from *Life of Lord Randolph Churchill*; John Milton, from Masson's *Life and Times of Milton*; William Blake, from *Life and Works of William Blake.*

Methuen & Co., Ltd., Sir John E. Millais, from *The Life and Letters of Sir John E. Millais*; Sir W. Raleigh, from *Selections from the Letters of Sir Walter Raleigh* (1880–1922); William Godwin, from *The Love Letters of Mary Hays*; G. K. Chesterton, Mrs. R. L. Stevenson, from *The Colvins and their Friends*; William Blake, from *Letters of William Blake.*

John Murray, Abraham Hayward and W. M. Thackeray, from *Selections from the Correspondence of Abraham Hayward*; Deane Swift, from *An Eighteenth-Century Correspondence*; Charles Darwin, from *The Life and Letters of Charles Darwin*; T. Creevey, from *The Creevey Papers*; Sir Frank Lockwood's sketch, from *The Life of Sir Frank Lockwood.*

Nonesuch Press, Ltd., Dr. Donne, from their edition of Donne's works.
Oxford University Press, Sir George Etherege, from *The Letterbook of Sir George Etherege.*
George Routledge & Sons, Ltd., John Bellows, from *The Letters of John Bellows*; Sara Coleridge, from *Memoir and Letters of Sara Coleridge.*
Elliot Stock, John Eliot, from *The New England Company.*
Lord Craigmyle, Lord Dunsany, Lord Moynihan, the Rt. Hon. Winston Churchill, Messrs. Maurice Baring, Oswald Barron, Arnold Bennett, G. W. Russell, George Sampson, George Bernard Shaw, George Slythe Street, for their letters.
Lt.-Col. the Hon. Benjamin Bathurst, letter from Queen Mary II.
Mr. Reginald Blunt, letter from Mrs. Vesey.
Mr. Basil Champneys, letters from Coventry Patmore.
China Inland Mission, letter from Mrs. Atwater.
Rt. Hon. Winston S. Churchill, letter from Lord Randolph Churchill.
Mrs. Clutton-Brock, letter from H. Clutton-Brock.
Mr. J. G. Commin, for selection from *The Paston Letters.*
Mrs. Conrad, letter from Joseph Conrad.
The Marquis of Crewe, letters from Lord Rosebery.
Sir Henry F. Dickens, as executor of Mrs. Kate Perugini, letters from Charles Dickens.
Miss Donaldson, letter from Lieut. Donaldson.
The Marquis of Dufferin and Ava, letters from Lady Dufferin.
Owners of copyright of George Eliot's letters, per Messrs. Ellis and Ellis.
Mrs. Eversden, letter from Lieut. Eversden.
Mrs. Hardy, letters from Thomas Hardy.
V. T. Harlow, letter from Sir William Codrington.
Mrs. E. M. Heath, letter from Lieut. Arthur Heath.
Mrs. Bernard Holland and Mr. Frank Holland, letters from Lady Mary Sibylla Holland.
Mr. Vyvyan Holland, letter from Oscar Wilde.
Lady Hulse, letter from Capt. Sir E. H. W. Hulse.
The Countess of Ilchester, letters from Lady Sarah Bunbury.
Mr. Gyles Isham, letter from Robert Tounson.
Mrs. Andrew Lang, letter from Andrew Lang.
Lt.-Col. the Hon. Rowland St. John, trustee of Miss Lockwood and the Hon. Mrs. Rowland St. John, for letters from Sir Frank Lockwood. London Missionary Society, letters from David Livingstone.
Mr. Eddie Marsh, letter from Rupert Brooke.
Mr. W. M. Meredith, letters from George Meredith.
Commander J. G. Millais, letter from Sir John Everett Millais.
Navy Records Society, letter from Sir Francis Drake.
Lord Newton, letters from Lord Lyons, and Sir Edward Malet.
L. H. Shore Nightingale, letter from Florence Nightingale.
Mr. Lloyd Osborne, letters from R. L. and Mrs. Stevenson.
Mrs. Josceline Otway, letter from Lord Nelson.
Mr. Herbert E. Palmer, letter from Lord Dunsany.
His Honour Sir Edward Parry, letters from Lady Dorothy Osborne and Sir William Temple.
Lady Richmond, letter from Gertrude Bell.
Mr. Archibald G. B. Russell, letters from William Blake.
Rev. H. Salter, Oxford Historical Society, letter from John James, published in *Letters of Radcliffe and James.*
Capt. D. M. Stanley, letters from Sir H. M. Stanley.
Mr. A. N. Tayler, for the Duff Letters.
Prof. G. M. Trevelyan, letters from Lord Macaulay.
Mr. C. A. Weekes, for G. W. Russell's letter.

CONTENTS

CONTENTS

THE FIVE HUNDRED BEST ENGLISH LETTERS

ALFRED THE GREAT (849–901)

At the age of twenty-two Alfred succeeded to a kingdom overrun by the Danes and in a state of constant war. By the end of his reign he had not only freed Southern England and given peace to the rest, but had found time, despite frequent illness, to reorganize the life of his country in every direction. His letter to Werferth, Bishop of Worcester, prefixed to his translation of Gregory's "Cura Pastoralis," shows how he laboured to remedy the ignorance which was a legacy of the Danish invasions.

TO BISHOP WERFERTH

King Alfred bids greet Bishop Waerferth with his words lovingly and with friendship. I would it be known to thee that it has very often come into my mind what wise men there formerly were throughout England, both church and lay folk, and how happy times there were then throughout England, and how the kings who had power over the nation in those days obeyed God and His ministers, and preserved peace, morality, and order at home, and at the same time, enlarged their territory abroad, and prospered both in war and in wisdom: and how zealous were God's ministers in teaching and in learning, and in all the services they owed Him: and how men came from oversea in search of wisdom and instruction, which we should now have to get from thence if we would have them. So far has it fallen in England that few there are on this side Humber who understand the English of their service or can translate a letter from Latin, nor are there many, I know, beyond Humber more learned. There were so few of them that I cannot remember one south of Thames when I first began to reign. God Almighty be thanked that we have any teachers among us now. And therefore I command thee, as I believe thou wouldst, to free thyself from worldly matters and apply the wisdom which God has given thee as thou art able. Consider what punishment shall fall upon us for the sake of this world, if we have neither loved wisdom ourselves nor suffered other men to obtain it; if we have loved the name of Christian only, and very few of us its duties.

When I considered all this I remembered how I had seen, before the land had been ravaged and burnt, how its churches stood filled with treasures and books, and with a multitude of His servants, but they had very little knowledge of the books, and could not understand them, for they were not written in their own language. As who should say: "Our forefathers who before us held these places, loved wisdom, and through it they obtained wisdom and left it to us. Here may we still see their footprints, but we cannot follow them up, and therefore have we lost both wealth and wisdom, since we would not incline our hearts to their example." When I remembered all this, I much marvelled that the good and wise men who were formerly all over England, and had perfectly learnt all these books, did not wish to translate them into their own tongue. But soon I answered myself and said: "They weened not that men should be so reckless and that learning would so decay; in that mind they forebore it, wishing that wisdom in this land might increase with our knowledge of languages." Then I remembered how the Law was first known in Hebrew, and after, when the Greeks had learned it, they translated it whole into their tongue, and all other books as well. And the Latins in turn, when they had learned it, translated the whole by learned interpreters into their own speech, and also all other Christian nations translated some part into their own language. Therefore it seems well to me, if ye think so, for us also to translate the books most needful for all men to know into the speech which all men know, and, as we are well able if we have peace, to make all the youth in England of free men rich enough to devote themselves to it, to learn while they are unfit for other occupation till they are well able to read English writing: and let those be afterwards taught Latin who are to continue learning and be promoted to higher rank.

When I remembered how Latin-learning had decayed in England, and yet many could read English, I began during the various and manifold troubles of this realm to translate into English the book which is called in Latin *Cura Pastoralis*, and in English "Shepherd's Book" sometimes word for word, and sometimes according to the sense, as I had learned it from Plegmund my archbishop, and Asser my bishop, and Grimbold and John my mass-priests. And when I had learned it as I could best understand and most clearly interpret it, I translated it into English; and I will send a copy to every bishopric in my kingdom; and on each there is a clasp worth 50 mancus [about £20]. And I command in God's name that no man take the clasp from the book or the book from the minster; it is uncertain how long there may be such learned bishops as now are, thanks be to God, nearly everywhere. Therefore I wish them always to remain in their place, unless the bishop wish to take them with him, or they be lent out anywhere, or any one make a copy from them.

HENRY VII (1457–1509)

The first of the great House of Tudor, Henry was the child of Edmund Tudor and Margaret Beaufort, Countess of Richmond. This letter shows the King at his best, not the miser nor the weakling who employed such agents as Empson and Dudley, but the affectionate son writing to his mother.

TO HIS MOTHER, MARGARET COUNTESS OF RICHMOND

MADAM, MY MOST ENTIRELY WELLBELOVED LADY AND MOTHER, I recommend me unto you in the most humble and lowly wise that I can, beseeching you of your daily and continual blessings. By your Confessor, the bearer, I have received your good and most loving writing, and by the same have heard at good leisure such credence as he would show unto me on your behalf, and thereupon have sped him in every behalf without delay, according to your noble petition and desire, which rests in two principal points: the one for a general pardon for all manner of causes: the other is for to alter and change part of a license which I had given unto you before, for to be put into mortmain at Westminster; and now to be converted into the University of Cambridge for your soul's health, etc. All which things, according to your desire and pleasure I have with all my heart and good will given and granted unto you. And, my Dame, not only in this but in all other things that I may know should be to your honour and pleasure and weal of your soul I shall be as glad to please you as your heart can desire it, and I know well that I am as much bounden so to do as any creature living, for the great and singular motherly love and affection that it has pleased you at all times to bear towards me. Wherefore, my own most loving mother, in my most hearty manner I thank you, beseeching you of your good continuance in the same. And Madam, your said Confessor has moreover shown unto me on your behalf that you, of your goodness and kind disposition, have given and granted unto me such title and interest as you have or ought to have in such debts and duties which is owing and due unto you in France, by the French King and others. Wherefore Madam in my most hearty and humble wise I thank you. Howbeit I verily think it will be right hard to recover it without it be driven by compulsion and force rather than by any true justice, which is not yet as we think any convenient time to be put in execution. Nevertheless, it has pleased you to give us a good interest and mean if they would not conform them to ransom and good justice to defend or offend at a convenient time when the case shall so require hereafter. For such a chance may fall that this your grant might stand in great stead for a recovery of our Right, and to make us free, whereas we be now bound. And verily, Madam, an I might recover it at this time or any other, you may be sure you should have your pleasure therein, as I and all that God has given me is and shall ever be at your will and commandment, as I have instructed Master Fisher more largely herein as I doubt not but he will declare unto you. And I beseech you to send me your mind and pleasure in the same, which I shall be full glad to follow with God's grace, which send and give unto you the full accomplishment of all your noble and virtuous desires. Written at Greenwich the 17th day of July, with the hand of your most humble and loving son

H. R.

After the writing of this letter, your Confessor delivered unto me such letters and writings obligatory of your duties in France which it has pleased you to send unto me, which I have received by an indenture of every parcel of the same. Wherefore, eftsoons in my most humble wise, I thank you, and I purpose hereafter, at better leisure, to know your mind and pleasure further therein. Madam, I have encumbred you now with this my long writing, but methinks that I can do no less, considering that it is so seldom that I do write. Wherefor I beseech you to pardon me, for verily, Madam, my sight is nothing so perfect as it has been; and I know well it will impair daily. Wherefore I trust that you will not be displeased though I write not so often with mine own hand, for on my faith I have been three days before I could make an end of this letter.

THE PASTON LETTERS

The Pastons were an old family of Norfolk. For a period of some eighty years—from 1424 to 1509—they kept their letters and household documents, and by a stroke of fortune similar to that which preserved to us Pepys's Diary, these letters have come down through the centuries. In them we see three generations playing their part in the world of the fifteenth century. In our selection we see the careful mother, old Agnes Paston; then comes pretty little Margery Brews, later to be Dame Paston herself. Few things ring more vividly from those dark days of the fifteenth century than Margery's love letter "unto my right well beloved Valentine."

AGNES PASTON TO JOHN PASTON

DWELLING IN THE INNER INN OF THE TEMPLE AT LONDON, BE THIS LETTER DELIVERED IN HASTE

SON, I greet you and send you God's blessing and mine. And as for my daughter your wife, she fares well, blessed be God, as a woman in her plight may do, and all your sons and daughters.

And forasmuch as ye will send me no tidings, I send you such as be in this country. Richard Linstead came this day from Paston and let me wot that on Saturday last past Dervale, half-brother to Waryn Harman, was taken with enemies, walking by the sea-side, and have him forth with them. And they took two pilgrims, a man and a woman, and they robbed the woman and let her go, and led the man to the sea, and when they knew he was a pilgrim they gave him money and set him again on the land. And they have this week taken four vessels off Winterton; and Hapisburgh and Eccles men be sore afraid for their taking of more, for there be ten great vessels of the enemies. God give grace that the sea may be better kept than it is now, or else it shall be a perilous dwelling by the sea coast.

I pray you greet well your brethren and tell them that I send them God's blessing and mine. And tell William that if Janet Lawton be not paid for the crimson cord which Alson Crane wrote to her for in her own name, that then he pay her and see Alson Crane's name struck out of her book. And I pray you that ye will remember the letter that I sent you last, and God be with you.

Written at Norwich, the Wednesday next before St. Gregory [March 11], 1450.

AGNES PASTON

AGNES PASTON TO JOHN PASTON

TO MY WELL BELOVED SON, BE THIS DELIVERED IN HASTE

SON, I greet you well and let you wit that forasmuch as your brother Clement letteth me wit that ye desire faithfully my blessing—that blessing that I prayed your father to give you the last day that ever he spake—and the blessing of all Saints under heaven, and mine might come to you all days and times. And think verily none other but that ye have it, and shall have it, with that, that I find you kind and willing to the weal of your father's soul, and to the welfare of your brethren.

By my counsel dispose yourself as much as ye may to have less to do in the world. Your father said: In little business lieth much rest. The world is but a thoroughfare, and full of woe; and when we depart therefrom right nought bare we with us but our good deeds and ill. And there knoweth no man how soon God will call him, and therefore it is good for every creature to be ready. Whom God visiteth him He loveth.

And as for your brethren they will, I know, certainly labour all that in them lieth for you. Our Lord have you in his blessed keeping, body and soul.

Written at Norwich the 29th day of October (1458)

By your mother,

A. P.

MARGERY BREWS UNTO MY RIGHT WELL BELOVED VALENTINE, JOHN PASTON, ESQUIRE,

BE THIS BILL DELIVERED

RIGHT reverend and worshipful and my right well beloved Valentine. I recommend me unto you full heartily, desiring to hear of your welfare, which I beseech Almighty God long for to preserve unto

His pleasure and your heart's desire. And if it please you to hear of my welfare, I am not in good hele of body nor of heart, nor shall be till I hear from you:

> For there wots no creature what pain that I endure
> And for to be dead I dare it not discure [discover].

And my lady my mother hath laboured the matter to my father full diligently, but she can no more get than ye know of; for the which God knoweth I am full sorry. But if that ye love me, as I trust verily that ye do, ye will not leave me therefor. For if that ye had not half the livelihood that ye have, for to do the greatest labour that any woman alive might I would not forsake you:

> And if ye command me to keep me true wherever I go
> I wiss I will do all my might you to love and never no mo
> And if my friends say that I do amiss
> They shall not me let (prevent) so for to do.
> Mine heart me bids ever more to love you
> Truly over all earthly thing
> And if they be never so wroth
> I trust it shall be better in time coming.

No more to you at this time, but the Holy Trinity have you in keeping. And I beseech you that this bill be not seen of none earthly creature save only yourself.

And this letter was indited at Topcroft, with full heavy heart

By your own
MARGERY BREWS

MARGERY PASTON TO MY MASTER, JOHN PASTON

RIGHT REVEREND AND WORSHIPFUL SIRE. In my most humble wise I recommend me to you, desiring to hear of your welfare, the which I beseech God to preserve to His pleasure, and so your heart's desire. Sir, I thank you for the venison that ye sent me; and your ship is sailed out of the haven as this day.

Sir, I send you by my brother William your stomacher of damask. As for your tippet of velvet, it is not here; Ann saith that ye put it in your casket at London.

Sir, your children be in good health, blessed be God.

Sir, I pray you send me the gold that I spake to you of, by the next man that cometh to Norwich.

Sir, your mast that lay at Yarmouth is let to a ship of Hull for

13*s.* 4*d.*, and if there fall any hurt thereto ye shall have a new mast therefore.

No more to you at this time, but Almighty God have you in His keeping. Written at Caistor, the 21st day of Janury in the first year of King Henry VII, (1486)

By your servant,
MARGERY PASTON

I pray God no ladies no more overcome you, that ye give no longer respite in your matters.

CARDINAL WOLSEY (1475–1530)

Few characters in the great cast of English history have played a more spectacular part than Cardinal Wolsey. The son of a poor Ipswich tradesman, by sheer adroitness and diplomacy he raised himself to be king of England in all but name, a Prince of the Church, the arbiter of fate far beyond the confines of his native land. But setting himself against his master Henry VIII in the matter of the Divorce he fell—more spectacular even in his fall than in his rise. One of the instruments that caused his disgrace was Thomas Cromwell, a creature of his own making; yet to him that proud nature was forced to condescend, even to write the following letter. Gardiner was another of his servants, yet see how he has to address him.

IN DISTRESS TO THOMAS CROMWELL

MINE OWN ENTIRELY BELOVED CROMWELL, I beseech you, as you love me and will ever do anything for me, repair hither this day, as soon as the Parliament is broken up, laying apart all things for that time; for I would not only communicate things unto you wherein for my comfort and relief I would have your good, sad, discreet advise and counsel, but also upon the same commit certain things requiring expedition to you, on my behalf to be solicited. This, I pray you therefore to haste your coming hither as afore, without omitting so to do as you, tender my succour, relief, and comfort, and quietness of mind. And thus fare you well: from Asher [Esher], in haste, this Saturday, in the morning, with the rude hand and sorrowful heart of your assured lover

T. CARDINALIS EBOR

I have also certain things concerning yourself which I am sure you will be glad to hear and know. Fail not, therefore, to be here this night, you may return early in the morning again if need shall so require. *Et iterum vale.*

M. Agustin shewed me how you had written unto me a letter wherein you should advise me of the coming hither of the Duke of Norfolk. I assure you there came to my hands no such letter.

My own good master Secretary, Going this day out of my pew to say mass, your letters dated yesternight at London were delivered unto me, by the continue whereof I understand that the King's Highness, of his excellent goodness and charity, is contented that I shall enjoy and have the administration of York, merely with the gifts of the promotions spiritual and temporal of the same: reserved only unto his noble Grace the gift of five or six of the best promotions: and that his pleasure is I shall leave Winchester and Saint Albans. As hereunto, Master Secretary, I cannot express how much I am bounden to the King's Royal Majesty for this his great and bounteous liberality, reputing the same to be much more than I shall ever be able to deserve. Howbeit, if his Majesty, considering the short and little time that I shall live in this world, by reason of such heaviness as I have conceived in my heart, with the destruction of the old houses, and the decay of the said archbishopric at the least to the sum of 800 marks yearly, by the reason of the Act passed for finish of testaments; with also my long painful service and poor degree; and for the declaration of his Grace's excellent charity, if his Highness be minded I shall leave Winchester and Saint Albans which I supposed, when I made my Submission, not offending in my truth towards his royal person, dignity or majesty royal, I should not now have deserved to have left; and much the more knowing his Grace's excellent propension to pity and mercy, and remembering of the frank parting with of all that I had in this world; that I may have some convenient pension reserved unto me, such as the King's Highness of his noble charity shall think meet. So ordering his that shall succeed and my living, that the same may be of like value yearly. Whereat my trust is and my heart so giveth me, that his Majesty would make no difficulty, if it may like you friendly to propose the same; assuring you that I desire not this for any mind, God is my judge, that I have to accumulate good, or desire that I have to the muck of the world; so God be thanked, at this hour, I set no more by the riches and promotions of the world than by the rush under my foot; but only for the declaration of the King's honour and his charity, and to have wherewith to do good deeds and to help my poor servants and kinsfolk. And furthermore that it would please the King's excellent goodness by your friendly mediation, considering how slenderly I am furnished in my house, now specially that the apparel of Winchester and Saint Albans shall be taken from me, to give and appoint unto me a convenient furniture for the same, *non ad pompam sed necessariam honestatem*: and if I may have the free gift and disposition of the benefices, it shall be greatly to my comfort. And yet when any of the five or six principal shall fortune to be void, the King's Grace being minded to have any of them, his Highness shall be as sure of the same as though they were reserved. And thus by his noble and merciful goodness delivered out of extreme calamity, and restored to a new freedom, I shall, with God's mercy and help, so order my life that I trust his Majesty shall take special comfort therein, and be pleased with the same. *Spero quod hæc quæ peto non videbuntur magna.* Howbeit I most humbly submit and refer all my petitions, *immo ipsam vitam*, to his gracious ordinance and pleasure, praying you to declare and signify the same, supplying mine indisposition and lack of wit conceived by reason of my extreme sorrow and heaviness, that the same may be to the King's contentation; whom I had rather be dead than offend in word, thought, or deed. And as touching the granting of the fee of £100 for Mr. Nores during his life for his good service done unto the King's Highness, for the which I have always loved him, and for the singular good heart and mind that I know he hath always borne unto me, I am content to make out my grant upon the same, if it would please the King to enlarge it to £100 more: and semblably, because Mr. Treasurer hath the keeping of the King's game nigh to Farnham, I would gladly if it may stand with the King's pleasure to grant unto him the reversion of such things as the Lord Sands hath there, with the amplification of the fee, above that which is oldly accustomed, to the sum of £40 by the year: and also I would gladly give to Mr. Controller a like fee: and to Mr. Russell another of £20 by the year: remitting this and all other my suits to the King's Highness pleasure, mercy, pity, and compassion most holy. Beseeching his Highness so now graciously to order me that I may from henceforth serve God quietly and with repose of mind, and pray as I am most bounden for the conservation and increase of his most noble and royal estate. And thus with my daily prayer I bid you farewell. From Esher hastily, with the rude hand and most heavy heart of your assured friend and bedesman.

T. CARDINALIS EBOR

TO THE RIGHT HONOURABLE
MR. SECRETARY, IN HASTE.

THE 5th EARL OF NORTHUMBERLAND (1478–1527)

In the North the Northumberlands were little short of royal in their power and the state they kept up. The following letters to Henry VIII give a vivid idea of the conditions of life in the Border country when England and Scotland were at daggers drawn.

[Mark Carr of Teviotdale and other Scots had boasted that they would come within] three miles of the poor house of Werkworth, where I lie, and give me light to put on my clothes at midnight; and also the said Mark Carr said there openly, that, seeing they had a governor of the Marches of Scotland, as well as they had in England, he should keep your highness's instructions, given unto your garrison, for making of any day-forrey [1]; for he and his friends would burn enough in the night, letting your council (i.e. the Privy Council) here define a notable act at their pleasure. Upon which, in your highness's name, I commanded due watch to be kept on your Marches, for coming in of any Scots. Nevertheless, upon Thursday at night, came thirty light-horsemen into a little village of mine called Whitell, having not more than six houses, lying towards Redesdale, upon Shilbottle more, and there would have fired the said houses, but there was no fire to get there, and they forgot to bring any with them . . .

And also I, by the advice of my brother Clifford, have devised that within this four nights, God willing, Kelso, in like case shall be burnt, with all the corn in the said town; and then they shall have no place to lie any garrison in nigh unto the Borders. And as I shall attain further knowledge, I shall not fail to satisfy your highness according to my most bounden duty. And this burning of Kelso is devised to be done secretly, by Tynedale and Redesdale. And thus the holy Trinity [keep] your most royal estate, with long life, and as much increase of honour as your most noble heart can desire. At Werkworth the xxiid day of October [1522].

[1] Henry had forbidden his garrison to make any flying raid or "day-foray" into Scotland.

The following letter, written in 1533, *gives the opposite side of the medal. It describes an attack on the Laird of Buccleugh's castle of Branksome, or Branxholm, by Northumberland's tenantry.*

MAY it please your most gracious highness to be informed that my comptroller, with Raynald Carnaby, desired licence of me to invade the realm of Scotland, for the annoyance of your highness's enemies, where they thought best exploit by them might be done, and to have to concur with them the inhabitants of Northumberland . . . as by their discretion upon the same they should think most convenient. And so they did meet upon Monday, before night, being the third day of this instant month, at Wauchope, upon North Tyne water . . . and before eleven of the clock did send forth a raiding-party of the men of Tynedale and Redesdale, and laid all the residue in ambush, and actively did set upon a town called Branxholme, where the Lord of Beuclough dwelleth. . . . Albeit, that night he was not at home . . . and thus scrymaged and frayed, supposing the Lord of Beuclough to be within three or four miles, to have led him into the ambush. And so in the breaking of the day did the forrey and the ambush meet, and recoiled homeward . . . And thus, thanks be to God, your highness's subjects, about the hour of twelve of the clock at noon the same day, came into this your highness's realm, bringing with them above eleven Scotsmen prisoners. . . . They brought also four hundred cattle and above nine horses and mares, keping in safety from loss or hurt all your said highness's subjects . . . Your highness's subjects were twelve miles within the ground of Scotland, and from my house at Werkworth is above nine miles of the most evil passage, where great snows do lie. Heretofore the same towns now burnt have not at any time in the mind of man in any wars been enterprised unto now. . . . Most humbly beseeching your majesty that your highness's thanks may concur unto them whose names be here inclosed, and to have in your most gracious memory the painful and diligent service of my poor servant Wharton, and thus, as I am most bounden, shall dispose it them that be under me for the annoyance of your highness's enemies.

SIR THOMAS MORE (1478–1535)

More was one of the tragedies of the Reformation. Learned, scrupulously just, of a delicate refinement, he embodied the most noble features of the Renaissance in England. Of a character far too staunch to bid his conscience obey a man-made ordinance, he suffered imprisonment and the ignominy of execution rather than waver for one moment in his allegiance to the Catholic Church. Two of his letters to Cardinal Wolsey show him at the height of his power; his letter to Margaret Roper, his faithful daughter, written from prison with pieces of charcoal, and her reply thereto, show the great man awaiting death.

TO CARDINAL WOLSEY

[1524]

IT may like your good Grace to be advertised that yesternight at my coming unto the King's Grace's presence, after that I had made your Grace's recommendations and his Highness showed himself very greatly glad and joyful of your Grace's health, as I was about to declare further to his Grace what letters I had brought his Highness, perceiving letters in my hand, prevented me ere I could begin, and said, "Ah you have letters now by John Joachim,[1] and I trow some resolution what they will do." "Nay verily, Sir," quoth I. "My lord has yet no word by John Joachim nor John Joachim, as far as my Lord knew, had yet no word himself this day in the morning when I departed from his Grace." "Nor had," quoth he; "I much marvel thereof, for John Joachim had a servant come to him two days ago." "Sir," quoth I, "if it like your Grace, this morning my Lord's Grace had nothing heard thereof; for yesterday his Grace at afternoon despatched me to your Grace with a letter sent from Doctor Knight, and the same night late, his Grace sent a servant of his to my house and commanded me to be with his Grace this morning by eight of the clock. Where at my coming he delivered me these other letters and advertisements send unto him from Mr. Pace, commanding me that after your Highness had seen them I should remit them to him with diligence, as well for

[1] A Genoese merchant employed by Francis I to negotiate a peace with England.

that he would show them to other of your Grace's council, as also to John Joachim, for the contents be such as will do him little pleasure." "Mary," quoth his Grace; "I am well paid thereof," and so he fell in merrily to the reading of the letters of Master Pace, and all the other abstracts and writings, whereof the contents as highly contented him as any tidings that I have seen come to him; and he thanked your Grace most heartily for your good and speedy advertisement. And forthwith he declared the news and every material point, which upon the reading his Grace well noted unto the Queen's Grace and all others about him, who were marvellous glad to hear it. And the Queen's Grace said that she was glad that the Spaniards had yet done somewhat in Italy in recompence of their departure out of Provence.

I showed his Highness that your Grace thought that the French King passed the mountains in hope to win all with a visage in Italy, and to find there no resistance: and his sudden coming much abashed the countries, putting each quarter in doubt of other and out of surity who might be well trusted. But now, since he finds it otherwise, missing the help of money which he hoped to have had in Milan; finding his enemies strong, and the fortresses well manned and furnished; and at Pavia, by the expugnation whereof he thought to put all the remainder in fear and dread, being now twice rejected with loss and reproach; his estimation shall so decay, and his friends fail, his enemies be confirmed and encouraged, namely such aid of the Germans of new joining with them that like, as the French King before wrote and boasted unto his mother that he had his own mind passed into Italy, so is it likely that she shall have shortly cause to write again to him that it had been much better and more wisdom for him to abide at home than to put himself there, whereas he stands in great peril whither ever he shall get thence. The King's Grace laughed and said that he thinks it will be very hard for him to get thence. And that he thinks the matters going thus, the Pope's Holiness will not be hasty neither in peace nor truce.

Upon the reading of Mr. Knight's letter his Grace said not much, but that if Burin come to his Grace he will be plain with him. And if he do not, but take his dispatch there of your Grace, which thing I perceive his Highness would be well content he did, except he desire to come to his presence, his Grace requires you so to talk with him as he may know that his Grace and you well perceive how the matters be handled by the emperor's agents in the enterprise.

The King's Grace is very glad that the matters of Scotland be in so good train, and would be loth that they were now ruffled by the Earl of Angus. And much his Highness allows the most prudent mind of your Grace, minding to use the Earl of Angus for an instrument to wring and wrest the matters into better train, if they walk awry, and not to wrestle with them and break them when they go right.

It may like your Grace also to be advertised that I moved his Grace concerning the suit of Mr. Broke in such wise as your Grace declared unto to me your pleasure, when Mr. Broke and I were with your Grace on Sunday. And his Grace answered me that he would take a breath therein, and that he would first speak with the young man; and then his Grace departed. But I perceived by his Grace that he had taken the young man's promise not to marry without his advice, because his Grace intended to marry him to some one of the Queen's maidens. If it would like your good Grace, in any letter which it should please your Grace hereafter to write hither, to make some mention and remembrance of that matter, I trust it would take good effect. And thus our Lord long preserve your good Grace in honour and health. At Hertford the 29th day of November.

Your Grace's humble orator and most bounden bedesman,

THOMAS MORE

TO THE SAME

IT may like your good Grace to be advertised that I have this night, after that the King's Grace had supped, presented and distinctly read unto his Highness as well your Grace's letter dated the 4th day of this present September addressed unto myself, as the four letters of the Queen of Scots, directed one to the King's Grace, and the other one to my Lord of Surrey; and also the two letters by your good Grace in the King's name most politically devised unto the said Queen of Scots. For which your labour, pain, travail, diligence, and study therein used, his Grace gave unto you his most affectionate thanks. And for as much as in the reading of my Lord of Surrey's letter directed unto your Grace, the King noted that my said Lord had already written unto the Queen of Scots answer unto both her said letters: his Grace requires you that it may like you to send him the copies which his letter specifies to have sent into your Grace.

His Grace also thinketh it right good that the Humes and Douglas be received upon convenient hostages; and that as well the Chancellor as the other Lords mentioned in the Queen's letter should be attempted by promises, gifts, and good policy to be won from the Duke and his faction.

And for as much as his Grace much desires in these things to be advertised of your most politic advice and counsel, which he thinks your Grace intends to declare by way of instructions to be given unto my said Lord of Surrey, his Highness therefore heartily requires your Grace that it may like the same to send to him the said instructions, that his Grace may by the same be learned of your Grace's prudent advise and counsel in the premises.

His Highness thinks it very necessary not only that my lord of Surrey were in all possible haste advertised of the declaration of the Duke of Bourbon, but also that the same were inserted within the letter which the Queen of Scots shall show to the Lords, with good exaggeration of the tyranny for which he renounces the French King and of the harm and ruin that is likely to fall to France thereby.

His Highness also requireth your Grace to weigh and consider the clause of the Queen's letter by which she desires with her trusty servants to be received into his realm, and how your high wisdom thinks good that matter to be ordered or answered. And to the intent in all these things your Grace may the more conveniently send him your most prudent advice, he has commanded me, with these presents, to remit all the said writings unto your good Grace, to be by your good Grace again sent into his Highness with your most politic counsel thereupon. And thus our Lord long preserve your good Grace in honour and health. Written at Woodstock the 22nd day of September, at midnight.

Your humble orator and most bounden bedesman,

THOMAS MORE

TO MARGARET ROPER

[1534]

MINE OWN GOOD DAUGHTER. Our Lord be thanked I am in good health of body, and in good quiet of mind: and of worldly things I no more desire than I have. I beseech Him make you all merry in the hope of heaven. And such things as I somewhat longed to talk with you all, concerning the world to come, our Lord put them into your minds, as I trust He doth, and better too, by His holy spirit: Who bless you and preserve you all. Written with a coal, by your tender loving father, who in his poor prayers forgetteth none of you all, nor your babes, nor your nurses, nor your good husbands, nor your good husbands' shrewd wives, nor your father's shrewd wife neither, nor our other friends. And thus fare ye heartily well, for lack of paper.

THOMAS MORE

Our Lord keep me continually true, faithful and plain, to the contrary whereof I beseech Him heartily never to suffer me live. For as for long life (as I have often told thee, Meg) I neither look for nor long for, but am well content to go, if God call me hence to-morrow. And I thank our Lord, I know no person living that I would had one fillip for my sake: of which mind I am more glad than of all the world.

Recommend me to your shrewd Will, and mine other sons, and to John Harris my friend, and yourself knoweth to whom else, and to my shrewd wife above all, and God preserve you all and make and keep you His servants all.

Margaret Roper replied thus:

[1534]

MINE OWN MOST ENTIRELY BELOVED FATHER. I think myself never able to give you sufficient thanks for the inestimable comfort my poor heart received in reading your most loving and godly letter, representing to me the clear shining brightness of your soul, the pure temple of the Holy Spirit of God, which I doubt not shall perpetually rest in you and you in Him. Father, if all the world had been given to me, as I be saved it had been a small pleasure in comparison of the pleasure I conceived of the treasure of your letter, which, though it were written with a coal, is worthy in mine opinion to be written in letters of gold. Father, what moved them to shut you up again, we can nothing hear. But surely I conjecture that when they considered that you were of so temperate a mind that you were contented to abide there all your life with such liberty, they thought it were never possible to incline you to their will, except it were by restraining you from the church, and the company of my good mother, your dear wife, and us your children and bedesfolk. But, father, this chance was not strange to you. For I shall not forget how you told us, when we were with you in the garden, that these things were like enough to chance you shortly after. Father, I have many times rehearsed to mine own comfort and divers other, your fashion and words that you had to us when we were last with you; for which I trust by the grace of God to be the better while I live, and when I am departed out of this frail life, which I pray God I may pass and end in His true obedient service, after the wholesome counsel and fruitful example of living I have had (good father) of you, whom I pray God give me grace to follow: which I shall the better, through the assistance of your devout prayers, the special stay of my frailty. Father, I am sorry I have no longer leisure at this time to talk with you, the chief comfort of my life; I trust to have occasion to write again shortly. I trust I have your daily prayer and blessing.

Your most loving obedient daughter and bedeswoman MARGARET ROPER, which daily and hourly is bound to pray for you, for whom she prayeth in this wise, that our Lord, of His infinite mercy, give you of His heavenly comfort, and so to assist you with His special grace, that ye never in any thing decline from His blessed will, but live and die His true obedient servant. Amen.

SIR BRIAN TUKE (*d.* 1545)

Sir Brian was the secretary to Henry VIII and appears to have done a good many unpleasant, if official, duties for him. Something of his zealousy in his master's cause can be gleaned from this letter to Cardinal Wolsey.

TO CARDINAL WOLSEY

PLEASE it, your good Grace, to understand. Ensuing the purpose which I last wrote unto your Grace, I sent one with my letters to Mr. Treasurer, for knowledge of the King's pleasure whither I should repair to his gracious presence. Which Mr. Treasurer, at the arrival of the messenger at Waltham, lay there sick of the sweat; and the King's highness removed to Hunsdon. The messenger followed, and, as I bade him in Mr. Treasurer's absence, he delivered the letters to the King, which his Grace read, both that which your Grace wrote to my Lord of London, my Lord of London's answer to me, and my letter to Mr. Treasurer. His Grace asked the messenger what disease I had, and he told his Grace wrong. Whereupon the King said I must needs come though I rode in a litter, and that if I had none his Grace would send me one. So, knowing his gracious pleasure, I followed on my mule at a footpace, with marvellous pain, insomuch, as I assure your Grace on my faith, I voided blood *per virgam*; and yesterday in the afternoon came hither, and spake with his Grace as soon as I came. His Highness seeming to be somewhat satisfied in the matter of the truce, by reason of the letters, said his first sending for me was for that cause, but now he must put me to another business, and occupy me here a good while; saying to me secretly, and willing me so to keep it, that it is to write out his last will, which his Highness hath now newly reformed.

His Highness having his supper on the board and in his sight, and being ready to sit down, would at that time dwell no more on the matter, but said he had himself provided my lodging at a gentleman's place nearby, and willed me to take my rest for that night, and to return to his Highness this day, at which time His Grace would confer with me upon the other said secret matter of his will. And so was willing to have rewarded me with a dish, if I had not said that I eat no fish; I, taking my leave of his Grace, departed two miles to the said lodging.

At my return this morning I found his Grace going to the garden, whither, by commandment of his Grace, I waited upon the same. After his return, and three Masses heard, his Highness immediately called me with him to a chamber that his Grace supped in apart yesternight; and after communication of the good state of this house, with the wholesomeness of the air, and how commodious it is for such a time of sickness as this is, with other things appertaining to those matters, his Highness delivered me the book of his said will in many points reformed, wherein his Grace examined me strictly, ordaining me a chamber here under his privy chamber, and willing me to send for my stuff and to go in hand with his business, and as I shall be in any doubt, to repair from time to time to his Grace. So if it be as they of the privy chamber tell me, I am not like to depart this five or six days at the least, though I have here no manner of stuff but a bed that I brought on horseback, ready to cast in an inn or house where I should fortune to come. Howbeit, I do send for my stuff and take in the mean time such as I can borrow; and am disappointed of my physic, which I had ordained to have used for a small time at my poor house in Essex, whither I sent a physician to remain with me for a season, promising him a mark a day, horsemeat and mansmeat. Now I would send him word to return till I may have leave to depart; at which time I do most humbly beseech your Grace to license me to attend upon my physician for eight or nine days, else I shall utterly, for lack of looking to this at the beginning, destroy myself forever.

It is said the King's highness will lie here eight or nine days. Other matters I have none worthy to advertise your Grace, whom I beseech Almighty God to preserve in good health, long life, and prosperity.

At Hunsdon, this Sunday, at dinner-time, the 20th day of June, 1528.

CATHERINE OF ARAGON (1485–1536)

The first ill-fated wife of Henry VIII, she knew a bitterness beyond that of most queens. After twenty years of matrimony he spurned her for the sake of flighty Anne Boleyn and she buried herself in the country to hide her grief and sorrow. Our letter was written in the height of her glory, when the news had just come of the victorious Battle of the Spurs.

TO THOMAS WOLSEY

August 25, 1513

Master Almoner, what comfort I have with the good tidings of your letter I need not write it to you, for the very reason that I have, showeth it. The victory hath been so great that I think none such hath been seen before. All England hath cause to thank God for it, and I specially, seeing that the King beginneth so well; which is to me a great hope that the end shall be like. I pray God to send the same shortly, for if this continue so still, I trust in him that everything shall follow thereafter to the King's pleasure and my comfort. Mr. Almoner, for the pain you take remembering to write to me so often, I thank you for it with all my heart, praying you to continue still sending me word how the King doeth, and if he keep still his good rule as he began. I think with the company of the emperor and with his good council his Grace shall not venture himself so much as I was afraid of before. I was very glad to hear of the meeting of them both, which hath been, to my seeming, the greatest honour to the King that ever came to Prince. The emperor hath done everything like himself. I trust to God he shall be thereby known for one of the most excellent princes in the world, and taken for another man than he was before thought. Mr. Almoner, I think myself that I am so bound to him for my part, that, in my letter, I beseech the King to recommend me unto him, and if his Grace thinketh that this shall be well done, I pray you to remember it. News from hence I have none; but such as I am sure the council have advertised the King of, and thereby you shall see how Almighty God helpeth here our part as well as there. I trow the cause is (as I hear say) that the King disposeth himself to him so well that I hope all shall be the better for his merits. And with this I make an end. At Richmond.

CATHERINE THE QUEEN

JOHN LONDON (*c.* 1486–1543)

When Henry VIII and Thomas Cromwell set about the Dissolution of the Monasteries they employed various trusty servants to cover the country and see that the good work was thoroughly carried out. Doctor London was one of their men and in this letter he tells of the "holy work" performed at Reading and Caversham.

TO LORD CROMWELL

In my most humble manner I have me commended to your Lordship, ascertaining the same that I have pulled down the image of Our Lady at Caversham whereunto was great pilgrimage. The image is plated over with silver, and I have put it in a chest fast locked and nailed up, and by the next barge that cometh from Reading to London it shall be brought to your Lordship. I have also pulled down the place she stood in, with all other ceremonies, such as lights, shrouds, crosses, and images of wax hanging about the chapel, and have defaced the same thoroughly, to prevent any further resort thither. This chapel did belong to Notley Abbey, and there always was a Canon of that monastery who was called the Warden of Caversham, and he sang in this chapel and had the offerings for his living. He was accustomed to show many pretty relics, among which were (as he made report) the holy dagger that killed King Henry and the holy knife that killed St. Edward. All these with many other, with the coats of this image, her cap and hair, my servant shall bring unto your Lordship this week, with a surrender of the friars under their convent seal, and their seal also.

I have seen the Canon home again to Notley and have made fast the door of the chapel, which is thoroughly well covered with lead; and if it be your Lordship's pleasure I shall see it made sure to the King's use. And if it be not so ordered, the chapel standeth so wildly that the lead will be stolen by night, as I was served at the friars. For as soon as I had taken the friars' surrender, the multitude of the poverty of the town resorted thither and all things that might be had they stole away; insomuch that they had conveyed the very clappers of the bells. And saving that Mr. Fachell, which made me great cheer at his house, and the Mayor did assist me, they would have made no little spoil. All this I have done as much as I could do to save everything to the King's use, as shall appear to your Lordship at the beginning of the term.

At Caversham is a proper lodging where the Canon lay, with a fair garden and an orchard meet to be bestowed on some friend of your Lordship in these parts; for the Canon had nothing to do there but to keep the chapel and receive the offerings.

I beseech your good Lordship to admit me a poor suitor for these honest men of Reading. They have a fair town and many good occupiers in it; but they lack that house necessary, of which for the ministration of justice they have most need of. Their Town Hall is a very small house and standeth upon the river where is the common washing place of the most part of the town; and in the Session days and other Court days there is such batting with battledores as one man cannot hear another nor the guest hear the charge-giving. The body of the church of the Grey Friars, which is ceiled with laths and lime, would be a very commodious room for them, and now that I have rid all that church of tabernacles, images and altars, it would make a goodly Town Hall. The mayor of this town, Mr. Roger Turner, a very honest gentle person, with many other honest men hath expressed unto me their grief in this behalf, and have desired me to be a humble suitor unto your Lordship for the same, if it should be sold. The walls, beside the quoin stones, be but chalk and flint, and the covering but tile, and if it pleases the King's grace to bestow that house upon any of his servants, he may spare the body of the church which standeth next to the street very well, and yet have room sufficient for a great man.

Your most bounden orator and servant,

JOHN LONDON

[The church was accordingly granted to the town as a Town Hall and in 1613 became a House of Correction.]

ARCHBISHOP THOMAS CRANMER (1489–1556)

Like many a man in high position in a time of transition, Cranmer, Archbishop of Canterbury, found himself torn betwixt the various claims of conscience, loyalty, and duty. His master the King had thrown off allegiance to his other master the Pope, and Cranmer was persuaded in his conscience that his duty lay with the former. Where it led him, and how he met his end at the stake, are too well known to need comment here. In this letter he describes a visit to Queen Catherine after her divorce and the coronation of her successor, Anne Boleyn.

TO NICHOLAS HAWKINS

In my most hearty wise I commend me unto you and even so would be right glad to hear of your welfare. . . . As touching the small determination and concluding of the matter of divorce between my Lady Catherine and the King's Grace, which said matter, after the Convocation in that behalf had determined and agreed according to the former consent of the universities, it was thought convenient by the King and his learned Council that I should repair unto Dunstable, which is within four miles unto Ampthill, where the said Lady Catherine keepeth her house, and there to call her before me to hear the final sentence in this said matter. Notwithstanding, she would not at all obey thereunto, for when she was by Dr. Lee cited to appear by a day, she utterly refused the same, saying that inasmuch as her cause was before the Pope, she would have none other judge; and therefore would not take me for her judge. Nevertheless the 8th day of May, according to the said appointment, I came unto Dunstable, my Lord [bishop] of Lincoln being assistant unto me and my Lord of Winchester, Dr. Bell, Dr. Claybroke, Dr. Tyrconnel, Dr. Hewis, Dr. Oliver, Dr. Brytten, Mr. Bedell, with divers others learned in the law being councillors in the law for the King's part. And so there, at our coming, we kept a court for the appearance of the said Lady Catherine, where were examined certain witnesses which testified that she was lawfully cited and called to appear, who for fault of appearance was declared contumacious. We proceeded in the said case against her *in poenam contumaciam*, as the processes of the law thereunto belongeth; which continued fifteen days after our coming thither. And the morrow after Ascension Day I gave final sentence therein, how that it was not dispensable for the Pope to license any such marriages.

This done, and after our journeying home again, the King's Highness prepared all things convenient for the coronation of the Queen [Ann Boleyn], which also was after such a manner as followeth.

The Thursday next before the Feast of Pentecost, the King and Queen being at Greenwich, all the crafts in London, thereunto well appointed in several barges decked after the most gorgeous and sumptuous manner, with divers pageants thereunto belonging, repaired and waited together upon the Mayor of London. And so, well furnished, came all unto Greenwich, where they tarried and waited for the Queen's coming to her barge. Which done, they brought her unto the Tower, trumpets, shawms, and other divers instruments playing all the way and making great melody, which, as is reported, was as comely done as never was like in any time nigh to our remembrance.

And so Her Grace came to the Tower on Thursday at night, about five of the clock, where also was such a peeling of guns as hath not been heard the like a great while before. And the same night and all day Friday the King and Queen tarried there; and on Friday at night the King made eighteen Knights of the Bath, whose creation was not only so strange to hear of as also their garments stranger to behold or look on. Which said knights, the next day, which was Saturday, rode before the Queen's grace throughout the City of London towards Westminster Palace, over and besides the most part of the nobles of the realm, which like accompanied Her Grace throughout the said city. She sat upon a horse litter richly apparelled and four Knights of the Cinque Ports bearing a canopy over her head. And after her came four rich chariots, one of them empty, and three others furnished with divers ancient old ladies; and after them came a great train of other ladies and gentlewomen. Which said progress from the beginning to the ending extended half a mile in length by estimation or there about. To whom also, as she came along the City, was shown many costly pageants with divers other encomiums spoken of children to her; wine also running at certain conduits plenteously. And so proceeding through the streets she passed forth unto Westminster Hall, where was a certain banquet prepared for her. Which done she was conveyed out to the back side of the Palace into a barge and so unto York Place, where the King's Grace was before her coming; for this you most ever presuppose that His Grace came always before her secretly in a barge, as well from Greenwich to the Tower as from the Tower to York Place.

Now, then, on Sunday was the Coronation, which also was of such a manner. In the morning there assembled with me at Westminster Hall the Bishop of York, the Bishop of London, the Bishop of Winchester, the Bishop of Lincoln, the Bishop of Bath, the Bishop of St. Asaph, the Abbot of Westminster, with ten or twelve more abbots, which all vested ourselves in our *pontificalibus*. And so furnished with our crosses and croisers, proceeded out of the Abbey in a procession unto Westminster Hall; where we received the Queen apparelled in a robe of purple velvet and all the ladies and gentlewomen in robes and gowns of scarlet according to the manner used beforetime in such business.

And so Her Grace, assisted on each side with two bishops, the Bishop of London and the Bishop of Winchester, came forth in procession unto the Church of Westminster, she in her hair, my Lord of Suffolk bearing before her a sceptre and a white rod. And so entered up unto the High Altar, where divers ceremonies used about her, I did set the crown on her head and then was sung Te Deum. And after that was sung a solemn Mass, all which while Her Grace sat crowned upon a scaffold which was made between the High Altar and the choir in Westminster Church. Which Mass and ceremonies done and finished, all the assembly of noblemen brought her unto Westminster Hall again, where she kept a great solemn feast all that day; the good order thereof were too long to write at this time to you.

But now, Sir, you may not imagine that this coronation was before her marriage, for she was married much about St. Paul's day last, as the condition thereof doth well appear by reason she is now somewhat big with child. Notwithstanding, it hath been reported through a great part of the realm that I married her; which was plainly false, for I myself knew not thereof a fortnight after it was done. And many other things be also reported of me which be mere lies and tales.

Other news have we none notable but that one Frith, which was in the Tower in prison, was appointed by the King's grace to be examined before me, my Lord of London, my Lord of Winchester, my Lord of Suffolk, my Lord Chancellor, and my Lord of Wiltshire, whose opinion was so notoriously erroneous that we again despatched him and were fain to leave him to the determination of his Ordinary which is the Bishop of London. His said opinion is of such nature that he thought it not necessary to be believed as an article of our Faith that there is the very corporeal presence of Christ within the Host and Sacrament of the Altar; and holdeth to this point most after the opinion of Oecolampadius. Surely I myself sent for him three or four times to persuade him to leave that his imagination, but for all that we could do therein he would not apply to any counsel, notwithstanding now that he is at a final end with all examinations; for my Lord of London hath given sentence and delivered him to the secular power, where he looketh every day to go unto the fire. And there is also condemned with him one Andrew, a tailor of London, for the said self-same opinion.

And thus fare you well, from my Manor of Croydon the 17th of June.

HENRY VIII (1491–1547)

Henry will always be remembered in England as the Father of the Reformation and the husband of six wives. Of his prowess as a warrior and a statesman but little can be said in so short a space, but the following two love-letters written to two successive wives depict him in another light.

TO ANNE BOLEYN

Mine own Sweetheart, this shall be to advertise you of the great melancholy that I find here since your departing; for, I ensure you, methinketh the time longer since your departing now last than I was wont to do a whole fortnight. I think your kindness and my fervency of love causeth it; for, otherwise I would not have thought it possible that for so little a while it should have grieved me. But now I am coming towards you, methinketh my pains by half removed; and also I am right well comforted insomuch that my book maketh substantially for my matter; in looking whereof I have spent above four hours this day, which causeth me now to write the shorter letter to you at this time, because of some pain in my head. Wishing myself (especially an evening) in my sweetheart's arms whose pretty duckies I trust shortly to kiss. Written by the hand of him that was, is, and shall be yours by his own will,

H. R.

TO JANE SEYMOUR

[1536]

My dear Friend and Mistress, The bearer of these few lines from thy entirely devoted servant will deliver into thy fair hands a token of my true affection for thee, hoping you will keep it for ever in your sincere love for me. Advertising you that there is a ballad made lately of great derision against us, which if it go much abroad and is seen by you, I pray you to pay no manner of regard to it. I am not at present informed who is the setter forth of this malignant writing, but if he is found out he shall be straitly punished for it. For the things ye lacked I have minded my lord to supply them as soon as he can buy them. Thus hoping shortly to receive you in these arms, I end for the present your loving servant and sovereign,

H. R.

ANNE BOLEYN (1507–36)

It was for Anne that Henry VIII gave up the wife with whom he had lived for twenty years; it was for Anne that he broke the hitherto unbroken allegiance of England to the Pope of Rome; it was for Anne that he braved the anger of the great powers of Europe. Yet it was this same Anne who, but two years after her marriage, was writing to her passionate lover the following heart-broken letter—while awaiting her death.

TO THE KING

Sir, Your Grace's displeasure and my imprisonment are things so strange unto me, as what to write, or what to excuse, I am altogether ignorant. Whereas you send unto me (willing [me] to confess a truth, and to obtain your favour) by such an one whom you know to be mine ancient professed enemy, I no sooner conceived this message by him, than I rightly conceived your meaning; and if, as you say, confessing a truth indeed may procure my safety, I shall with all willingness and duty perform your command.

But let not your Grace ever imagine that your poor wife will ever be brought to acknowledge a fault where not so much as a thought thereof proceeded. And to speak a truth, never prince had wife more loyal in all duty, and in all true affection, than you have ever found in Anne Boleyn; with which name and place I could willingly have contented myself, if God and your Grace's pleasure had been so pleased. Neither did I at any time so far forget myself in my exaltation or received queenship, but that I always looked for such an alteration as now I find: for the ground of my preferment being on no surer foundation than your Grace's fancy, the least alteration I knew was fit and sufficient to draw that fancy to some other subject. You have chosen me from a low estate to be your queen and companion, far beyond my desert or desire. If then you found me worthy of such honour, good your Grace, let not any light fancy or bad counsel of mine enemies withdraw your princely favour from me; neither let that stain, that unworthy stain, of a disloyal heart towards your good Grace, ever cast so foul a blot on your most dutiful wife, and the infant princess, your daughter.

Try me, good king, but let me have a lawful trial; and let not my sworn enemies sit as my accusers and my judges; yea, let me receive an open trial, for my truth shall fear no open shame. Then shall you see either mine innocency cleared, your suspicions and conscience satisfied, the ignominy and slander of the world stopped, or my guilt openly declared; so that, whatsoever God or you may determine of me, your Grace may be freed from an open censure; and mine offence being so lawfully proved, your Grace is at liberty, both before God and man, not only to execute worthy punishment on me, as an unlawful wife, but to follow your affection already settled on that party for whose sake I am now as I am, whose name I could some good while since have pointed unto; your Grace not being ignorant of my suspicion therein.

But if you have already determined of me; and that not only my death, but an infamous slander, must bring you the enjoying of your desired happiness; then I desire of God that he will pardon your great sin therein, and likewise my enemies the instruments thereof; and that He will not call you to a strict account for your unprincely and cruel usage of me, at his general judgment-seat, where both you and myself must shortly appear; and in whose judgment, I doubt not, whatsoever the world may think of me, mine innocence shall be openly known and sufficiently cleared.

My last and only request shall be, that myself may only bear the burden of your Grace's displeasure, and that it may not touch the innocent souls of those poor gentlemen who, as I understand, are likewise in strait imprisonment for my sake. If ever I have found favour in your sight, if ever the name of Anne Boleyn hath been pleasing in your ears, then let me obtain this request; and I will so leave to trouble your Grace any further; with mine earnest prayers to the Trinity, to have your Grace in his good keeping, and to direct you in all your actions. From my doleful prison in the Tower, this 6th of May. Your most loyal and ever faithful wife,

Anne Boleyn

ROGER ASCHAM (1515–68)

Ascham was one of the greatest classical scholars Cambridge has ever produced. He was tutor to Princess Elizabeth when she was a girl, and in later years served as Latin secretary to Mary and his old pupil.

TO BISHOP GARDINER

[April 1554]

In writing out my patent I have left a vacant place for your wisdom to value the sum; wherein I trust to find further favour; for I have both good cause to ask it, and better hope to obtain it, partly in consideration of my unrewarded pains and undischarged costs in teaching King Edward's person, partly for my three years' service in the Emperor's court, but chiefly of all when King Henry first gave it me at Greenwich, your lordship in the gallery there asking me what the king had given me, and knowing the truth, your lordship said it was too little, and most gently offered me to speak to the king for me. But then I most happily desired your lordship to reserve that goodness to another time, which time God hath granted even to these days, when your lordship may now perform by favour as much as then you wished by good will, being as easy to obtain the one as to ask the other. And I beseech your lordship see what good is offered me in writing the patent: the space which is left by chance doth seem to crave by good luck some words of length, as *viginti* or *triginta*, yea, with the help of a little dash *quadraginta* would serve best of all. But sure as for *decem* it is somewhat with the shortest; nevertheless I for my part shall be no less contented with the one than glad with the other, and for either of both more than bound to your lordship. And thus God prosper your lordship.

Your lordship's most bounded to serve you,

R. Askham

TO HIS WIFE MARGARET

[November 1568]

Mine own good Margaret,—The more I think upon your sweet babe, as I do many times both day and night, the greater cause I always find of giving thanks continually to God for his singular goodness bestowed at this time upon the child, yourself, and me, even because it hath rather pleased him to take the child to himself into heaven, than to leave it here with us still on earth. When I mused on the matter, as nature, flesh, and fatherly fantasy did carry me, I found nothing but sorrows and care, which very much did vex and trouble me, but at last forsaking these worldly thoughts, and referring me wholly to the will and order of God in the matter, I found such a change, such a cause of joy, such a plenty of God's grace towards the child, and of his goodness towards you and me, as neither my heart can comprehend, nor yet my tongue express the twentieth part thereof.

Nevertheless, because God and good will hath so joined you and me together as we must not only be the one a comfort to the other in sorrow, but also partakers together in any joy, I could not but declare unto you what just cause I think we both have of comfort and gladness by that God hath so graciously dealt with us as he hath. My first step from care to comfort was this, I thought God had done his will with our child, and because God by his wisdom knoweth what is best, and by his goodness will do best, I was by and by fully persuaded the best that can be is done with our sweet child, but seeing God's wisdom is unsearchable with any man's heart, and his goodness unspeakable with any man's tongue, I will come down from such high thoughts, and talk more sensibly with you, and lay open before you such matter as may be both a full comfort of all our cares past, and also a just cause of rejoicing as long as we live. You well remember our continued desire and wish, our nightly prayer together, that God would vouchsafe to us to increase the number of this world; we wished that nature should beautifully perform the work by us; we did talk how to bring up our child in learning and virtue; we had care to provide for it, so as honest fortune should favour and follow it. And see, sweet wife, how mercifully God hath dealt with us in all points, for what wish could desire, what prayer could crave, what nature could perform, what virtue could deserve, what fortune could afford, both we have received, and our child doth enjoy already. And because our desire (thanked be God) was always joined with honesty, and our prayers mingled with fear, and applied always to the world too, the will and pleasure of God hath given us more than we wished, and that which is better for us now than we could hope to think upon; but you desire to hear and know how many, even thus, we desired to be made vessels to increase the world, and it hath pleased God to make us vessels to increase heaven, which is the greatest honour to man, the greatest joy to heaven, the greatest spite to the devil, the greatest sorrow to hell, that any man can imagine. Secondarily, when nature had performed what she would grace stepped forth and took our child from nature, and gave it such gifts over and above the power of nature, as where it could not creep in earth by nature it was straitway well able to go to heaven by grace. It could not then speak by nature, and now it doth praise God by grace; it could not then comfort the sick and careful mother by nature, and now through prayer is able to help father and mother by grace; and yet, thanked be nature, that hath done all she could do, and blessed be grace that hath done more and better than we would wish she should have done. Peradventure yet you do wish that nature had kept it from death a little longer, yea, but grace hath carried it where now no sickness can follow, nor any death hereafter meddle with it; and instead of a short life with troubles on earth, it doth now live a life that never shall end with all manner of joy in heaven.

And now, Margaret, go to, I pray you, and tell me as you think, do you love your sweet babe so little, do you envy his happy state so much, yea, once to wish that nature should have rather followed your pleasure in keeping your child in this miserable world, than grace should have purchased such profit for your child in bringing him to such felicity in heaven? Thirdly, you may say unto me, if the child had lived in this world, it might have come to such goodness by grace and virtue as might have turned to great comfort to us, to good service to our country, and served to have deserved as high a place in heaven as he doth now. To this, in short, I answer, ought we not in all things to submit to God's good will and pleasure, and thereafter to rule our affections, which I doubt not but you will endeavour to do? And therefore I will say no more, but with all comfort, to you here, and a blessing hereafter, which I doubt not but is prepared for you.

Your dearly loving husband,

Roger Askam

ELIZABETH (1533–1603)

The glory and pride of England and the wonder of the civilized world, Elizabeth, the Virgin Queen, to whom the wits and geniuses of England turned in reverend awe and admiration, was herself no mean scholar. The first letter printed below was written to her sister the Queen, from Hatfield, a few months before Mary's death. The other, written to James VI of Scotland—himself to be King of England in later years—upbraiding him with breaking his word, reveals something of her mind.

TO QUEEN MARY

LIKE as the riche[1] man that dayly gathereth riches to riches, and to one bag of money layeth a greate sort til it come to infinit, so me thinkes, your Maiestie not beinge suffised with many benefits and gentilnes shewed to me afore this time, dothe now increase them in askinge and desiring wher you may bid and comaunde, requiring a thinge not worthy the desiringe for it selfe, but made worthy for your highness request. My pictur I mene, in wiche if the inward good mynde towarde your grace might as wel be declared as the outwarde face and countenance shal be seen, I wold nor haue taried the comandement but prevent it, nor haue bine the last to graunt but the first to offer it. For the face, I graunt, I might wel blusche to offer, but the mynde I shall neur be ashamed to present. For thogth from the grace of the pictur, the coulers may fade by time, may giue by wether, may be spotted by chance, yet the other nor time with her swift winges shall ouertake, nor the mistie cloudes with their loweringes may darken, nor chance with her slipery fote may overthrow. Of this althogth yet the profe could not be greate because the occasions hathe bine but smal, notwithstandinge as a dog hathe a day, so may I perchaunce haue time to declare it in deeds wher now I do write them but in wordes. And further I shal most humbly beseche your Maiestie that whan you shall loke on my pictur you wil witsafe to thinke that as you haue but the outwarde shadow of the body afore you, so my inward minde wischeth, that the body it selfe wer oftener in your presence; howbeit bicause bothe my so beinge I thinke coulde do your Maiestie

[1] This letter has been left in Elizabeth's own spelling.

litel pleasure thogth my selfe great good, and againe bicause I se as yet not the time agreing therūto, I shal lerne to folow this sainge of Orace, Feras non culpes quod vitari non potest. And thus I wil (troblinge your Maiestie I fere) ende with my most humble thankes, besechinge God longe to preserue you to his honour, to your cōfort, to the realmes profit, and to my joy. From Hatfilde this 1 day of May.

Your Maiesties most humbly Sistar and Seruante,

ELIZABETH

TO KING JAMES THE SIXTH OF SCOTLAND

[AUGUST 7, 1583]

AMONG your many studies my dear Brother and Cousin, I would Isocrates's noble lesson were not forgotten, that wills the Emperor his sovereign to make his words of more account than other men their oaths, as meetest ensigns to show the truest badge of a Prince's arms. It moveth me much to move you, when I behold how diversely sundry wicked paths, and, like all evil illusions, wrapped under the cloak of your best safety, endanger your state and best good. How may it be that you can suppose an honourable answer may be made me when all your doings gainsay your former vows. You deal not with one whose experience can take dross for good payments, nor one that easily will be beguiled. No, no, I mind to set to school your craftiest counsellor. I am sorry to see you bent to wrong yourself in thinking to wrong others; there are those which if they had not even then taken opportunity to let a ruin that was newly begun, that plot would have perilled you more than a thousand of such mean lives be worth, that persuade you to vouch such deeds to deserve a soul's pardon. Why do you forget what you write to myself with your own hand, showing how dangerous a course the Duke was entered in, though you excused himself to think no harm therein, and yet they that with your safety preserved you from it, you must seem to give them reproach of guilty folk. I hope you more esteem your honour than to give it such a stain, since you have protested so often to have taken these Lords for your most affectionate subjects, and to have done all for your best. To conclude, I beseech you pass no further in this cause till you receive an express messenger, a trusty servant of mine, by whom you shall see plainly how you may receive honour and contentment with more surety to your rest and state, than all these dissembling counsellors will or can bring you. As knoweth the Lord to whose most sage keeping I do commit you, with my many commendations to your person.

WILLIAM FLEETWOOD (*c.* 1535–94)

Fleetwood was a London man and was made Recorder in 1571. *His description of festivities over three hundred years ago shows how loyal the City is to its old traditions.*

TO LORD BURGHLEY

[JULY 18, 1583]

RIGHT HONOURABLE,

Since your Lordship's last being here in London there have been two great feasts, the one at the Grocer's Hall, the other at the Haberdashers' Hall. At the Haberdashers' feast was my Lord Mayor, and divers of his brethren with myself, where my Lord Mayor after the second course came in, did take the great standing-cup of the gift of Sir William Garrett, being full of hypocras (and silence being commanded through all the tables) all men being bare-headed, My Lord before all men did use these words, with a convenient loud voice: "Mr. Recorder of London, and you my good brethren the Aldermen, bear witness that I do drink unto Mr. Alderman Massam as Sheriff of London and Middlesex from Michaelmas next coming for one whole year; I do beseech God to grant him as quiet and peaceable a year, with as good and gracious favour of Her Majesty, as I myself and my brethren the Sheriffs now being have hitherto had, and as I trust shall have." This spoken all men desired the same. The sword-bearer in haste went to the Grocers' feast, where Mr. Alderman Massam was at dinner, and there did openly declare the words that my Lord Mayor had used. Whereunto, (silence made and all being hushed), the Alderman answered very modestly in this sort, "First, I thank God, who through his great goodness hath called me from a very poor and mean degree unto this worshipful estate. Secondly, I thank Her Majesty for her gracious goodness in allowing unto us these great and ample franchises. Thirdly, I thank my Lord Mayor for having so honourable an opinion of this my Company of Grocers as to make choice of me, being a poor member of the same." And this said, both he and the Company, pledged my Lord and gave him thanks.

Mr. Nowell of the Court hath lately been here in London. He

caused his man to give a blow unto a carman. His man hath stricken the carman with the pummel of his sword and therewith has broken his skull and killed him. Mr. Nowell and his man are like to be indicted; whereof I am sure to be much troubled, what with letters and his friends, and what by other means, as in the very like case heretofore I have been even with the same man. Here are sundry young gentlemen that use the Court that most commonly term themselves *gentlemen*. When any of these have done anything amiss and are complained of, or arrested for debt, they then run unto me, and no other excuse or answer can they make but say, "I am a gentleman, and being a gentleman I am not thus to be used at a slave and cullion's hands." I know not what other parley Mr. Nowell can plead; but this I say, the fact is foul. God send them good deliverance. I think in my conscience that he maketh no reckoning of the matter.

It was my chance to examine a matter in the Court held at Bridewell. I have been complained of to the Council Board. I was sent for. Mr. Secretary received my answer and told the complainants that they deserved to be hanged. This is the case. Abraham of Abraham, a gentleman of a hundred pounds land in Lancashire, put his daughter and heiress unto my Lady Gerrerd. Sir Thomas and my Lady being here in London, one Dwelles, a fencer, and his wife, by indirect means, being of kin to the girl, did invite all my Lady's children and gentlewomen unto a breakfast. They came thither and at their coming the youths and serving-men were carried up to the Fence School. My Lady's daughters and gentlewomen must needs play at cards, will they nill they. The girl Abraham, by the wife of the house was conveyed into a chamber and shut the door after her and there left her. The girl found in the chamber four or five tall men. She knew them not. And immediately the girl fell into a great fear, seeing them to compass her about. Then began an old priest to read upon a book; his words she understood not, saving these words, "I, Henry, take thee, Susan, to my wedded wife," etc. This done they charged the wench never to discover [reveal] this to anybody alive; and so sent her down to her fellows. And dinner being done the wench told her fellows very lamentably what had been done; and they over to Sir Thomas and my Lady. And upon complaint I sent for the fencer's wife who would confess nothing. I went with her myself to Bridewell, where there was a full court, and thither came Sir Thomas with the wench, and there we bolted out the whole matter and did no more. The fencer's wife is returned to the compter. The wench is with my Lady Gerrerd. She was never in Bridewell, as the fencer and one Poollwhele did avouch to some of my lords. The wench was there to accuse the fencers' wife in open court. My Lord, this being the fact and the true case thereto, I find the same to be felony; therefore methinketh such companions as this fencer and his wife ought not to be allowed to defame such poor men as I am, in such order; before the Lords. Thus most humbly I take my leave of your good Lordship, this 18 July, 1583.

W. FLEETWOOD